2/15

W9-BUR-031

Mechanic Mike's Machines

Trains

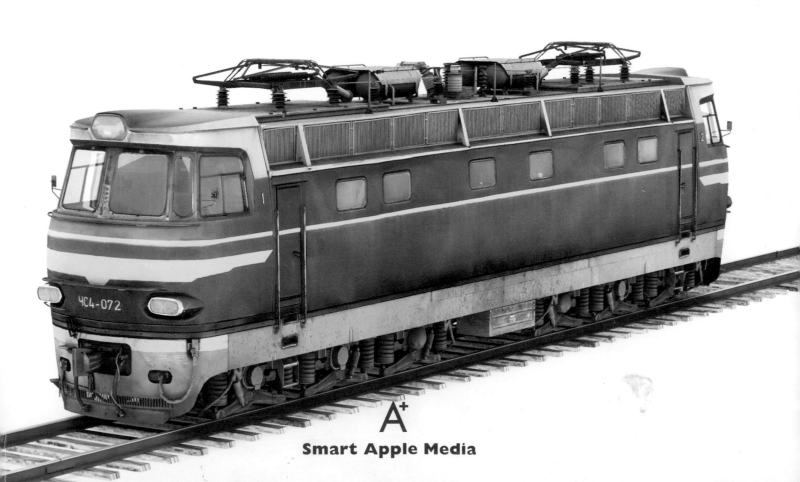

A+

Smart Apple Media

Published by Smart Apple Media, an imprint of Black Rabbit Books
P.O. Box 3263, Mankato, Minnesota 56002
www.blackrabbitbooks.com

Produced by David West ⚇ Children's Books
6 Princeton Court, 55 Felsham Road, London SW15 1AZ

Designed and illustrated by David West

Cataloging-in-Publication data is available from the Library of Congress.
West, David, 1956- author.
 Trains / David West.
       pages cm – (Mechanic Mike's machines)
Summary: "This new title introduces young readers to trains. Starting with the original steam powered
locomotive, this title teaches young readers all about different trains that have developed. Large-scale
pictures accompany a description of each train and are complemented by sidebars containing
interesting facts"–Provided by publisher.
Includes index.
Audience: K-3
ISBN 978-1-62588-060-4 (library binding)
ISBN 978-1-62588-099-4 (paperback)
1.   Railroad trains–Juvenile literature.   I. Title. II. Series: West, David, 1956- Mechanic Mike's machines.
TF148.W469 2015
625.2–dc 3
                                                                                              2013031985
Printed in China
CPSIA compliance information: DWCB14CP
010114
9 8 7 6 5 4 3 2 1

Mechanic Mike says:
This little guy will tell you something more about the machine.

Find out what type of engine drives the machine.

Discover something you didn't know.

Is it fast or slow? Top speeds are given here.

How many crew or people does it carry?

Get your amazing fact here!

Contents

Early American steam **locomotives** like the "General," built in 1855, had a tall chimney stack and a cow catcher on the front. This was to clear the rail line of anything that might derail the train.

Early steam trains, such as the "General," could reach 20 mph (32.1 km/h) in short bursts.

Steam trains usually had a crew of at least two people. The driver and the fireman who kept the fire in the boiler fed with coal.

Did you know the "General" is famous for its part in the "Great Locomotive Chase" during the Civil War? Union raiders stole the train and were chased by Confederates in other trains.

It has a steam engine.

Steam

The earliest locomotives were powered by steam. Coal or wood was burned to heat up water in a boiler to make steam.

Mechanic Mike says:
Steam from the boiler pushed pistons inside cylinders. The rods attached to the pistons turned the wheels.

W. & A. R. R.

3

The biggest **diesels** ever built were the Union Pacific Centennial locomotives. They were 98 feet, 5 inches (30 m) long.

Diesel trains can be fast and powerful. The high-speed diesel train, InterCity 125, used for passenger service in the UK is the fastest diesel train at 144 mph (231 km/h).

A former Santa Fe F45, in Montana, has been converted into a lodge where up to four people can stay.

This diesel-electric EMD F45 has a crew of two.

This EMD F45 has a 20 cylinder diesel engine powering electric motors.

Mechanic Mike says:
Diesel trains that power electric motors are sometimes called diesel-electric trains.

Diesel

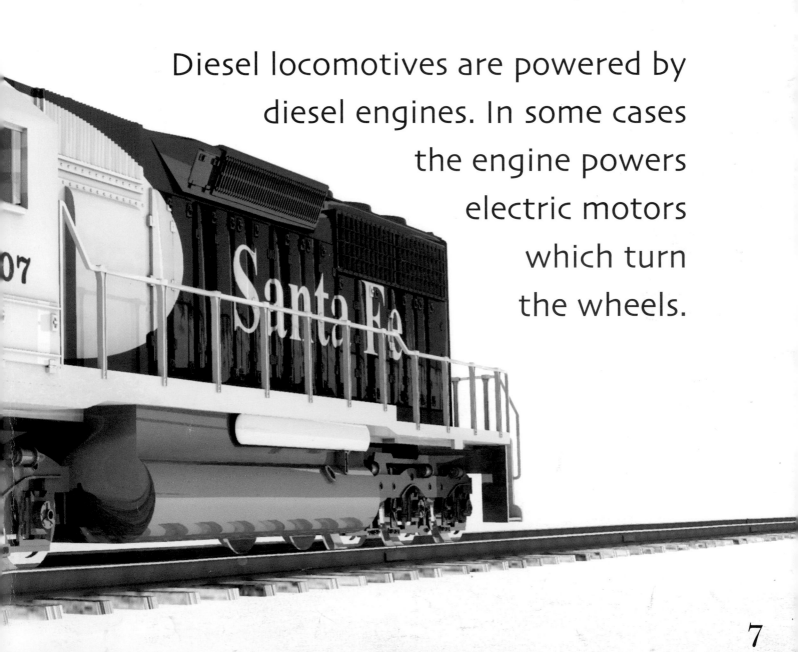

Diesel locomotives are powered by
diesel engines. In some cases
the engine powers
electric motors
which turn
the wheels.

Electric

Electric locomotives are powered by electricity from a third rail or from overhead lines. Flexible rods called pantographs on the roof of the locomotive contact the overhead wire to transfer the electricity.

Mechanic Mike says:
At the flick of a switch this locomotive can travel forward or backward.

This ChS4-012 pulled passenger carriages between Moscow and Odessa, in Russia.

 Although electric locomotives can be fast, this Russian Skoda ChS4's top speed is 99 mph (160 km/h).

 The latest version of this locomotive can pull 32 passenger carriages.

 Did you know that the ChS4-012 has been retired and can be seen in the Kiev museum of railway transport?

It is powered by electric motors.

9

High-Speed

High-speed trains carry passengers on
special tracks over long distances
at speeds of around 200 mph
(320 km/h).

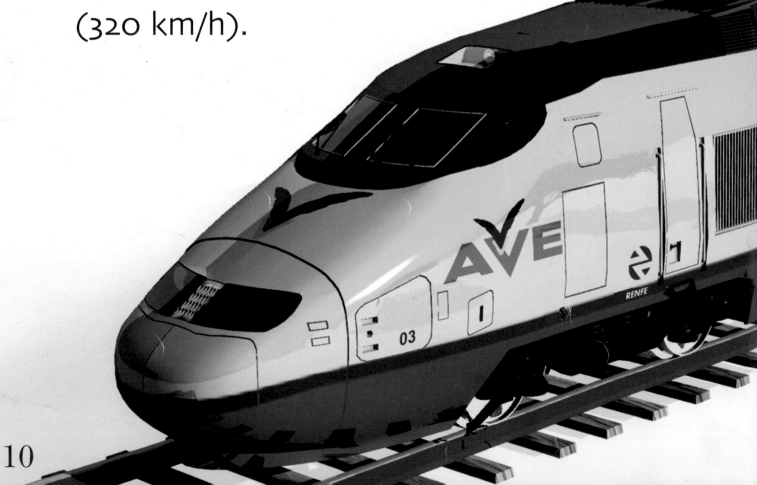

The Chinese CRH380A is the fastest high-speed train in operation. It is designed to travel at 217 mph (350 km/h).

 It is powered by electric motors.

 High-speed trains require only one driver.

 Did you know that the French TGV set a speed record of 357.2 mph (574.8 km/h)?

 This Spanish high-speed train can achieve speeds of up to 193 mph (310 km/h) on runs between Madrid and Seville.

Mechanic Mike says:
China has the world's longest high-speed rail line, which runs 1,372 miles (2,208 km) from Beijing in the north to Shenzhen on the southern coast.

11

Freight

Trains don't just carry people. They are an economical way of transporting all sorts of goods from oil, gas, and coal to grain, cattle, and ore.

Mechanic Mike says:
In some countries rolling highway trains are used. These freight trains have special wagons that allow trucks to drive straight onto the train and drive off again when the destination is reached.

Did you know the Daqin Railway in China transports more than 1.1 million tons (1 million tonnes) of coal to the east seashore every day?

Freight trains are usually limited to around 75 mph (120.7 km/h).

Loads can be 145 tons (130 tonnes) per wagon and tens of thousands of tons per train.

Freight trains are normally pulled by diesel locomotives.

Some freight trains can be over 4.3 miles (7 km) long.

The first **rapid transit system** was the London Underground, which opened in 1863.

 Did you know that the busiest rapid transport systems in the world are the Tokyo subway, the Seoul Metropolitan Subway, and the Moscow Metro? The New York City Subway has the record for the most stations.

 The train's top speed is 50 mph (80 km/h), while the average speed is **25 mph** (40 km/h).

 The Danish Copenhagen metro system carries over 137,000 people per day. Each three-carriage train holds up to 96 seated and 204 standing passengers.

 The train is powered by electric motors. The electricity is picked up from a third electrified rail.

Rapid Transit

Rapid transit trains carry passengers around **urban** areas. The trains run frequently and are designed to carry lots of people. They often travel on lines above roads and underground.

Mechanic Mike says:
Some rapid transit trains, like this Copenhagen Metro in Denmark, are completely automated and have no driver.

The Colorado Rail Bilevel rail cars are 19.75 feet (6 m) tall.

Did you know that some countries, such as the UK, don't have bilevel trains since they won't fit under many of the bridges?

Some high-speed bilevel trains can travel over 100 mph (160 km/h).

A four-car set can carry around 400 people.

This is a multiple unit train consisting of self-propelled carriages, using electricity to drive electric motors in many of the carriages.

Bilevel

Mechanic Mike says:
Bilevel trains can be seen in many countries around the world. This one runs in the Netherlands.

These tall trains, also known as double-deckers, have two levels for passengers. This allows them to carry more people in a shorter train. A longer train would need longer platforms to be built.

Tram

These rail vehicles run on tracks along city streets, and sometimes on special rail lines as well. Most trams today use electrical power, usually supplied by a pantograph.

The very first tram was horse-drawn. It first ran in 1807, in South Wales in the UK, between Swansea and the Mumbles.

Did you know that some trams, called cable cars, are pulled by cables?

Modern trams may be up to 236 feet (72 m) long and carry 510 passengers.

Most modern trams are powered by electric motors.

Mechanic Mike says: Trams are also known as trolleys, or streetcars.

Trams are limited to a speed limit depending on the country. It is generally around 50 mph (80 km/h).

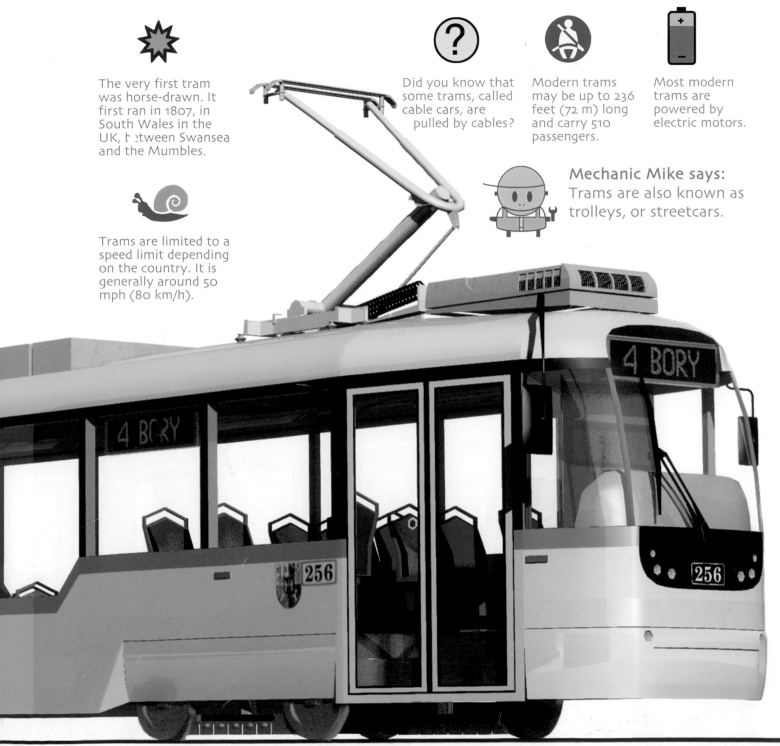

Some monorail designs have the trains suspended from a single rail rather than sitting on top of it.

Monorails are generally quite slow. The Tokyo Monorail runs at 50 mph (80 km/h).

The first monorail to carry passengers operated during the 1820s in Hertfordshire, in the UK.

The busiest monorail line is the Tokyo Monorail. It carries more than 300,000 passengers daily.

Almost all modern monorails are powered by electric motors.

Mechanic Mike says:
Monorails like this one in Las Vegas are popular with tourists, as the height gives them a more **elevated** view of the city.

20

Monorail

These trains run along one rail which is usually high above the ground. The train has rubber wheels which can grip the monorail, allowing it to go up and down slopes.

Maglev

Maglev trains use powerful **electromagnets** to hover above the rail. The magnets are also used to move the train. As there is no contact with the rail, these trains are very smooth, quiet, and fast.

SNT

The first commercial maglev train was called "MAGLEV" and opened in 1984 near Birmingham, in the UK.

 The highest recorded speed of a maglev train is 361 mph (581 km/h).

 The top operational speed of this Shanghai Maglev train is 268 mph (431 km/h), making it the world's fastest train in regular use.

 The Shanghai Maglev can carry 244 people.

 It uses electromagnetic propulsion.

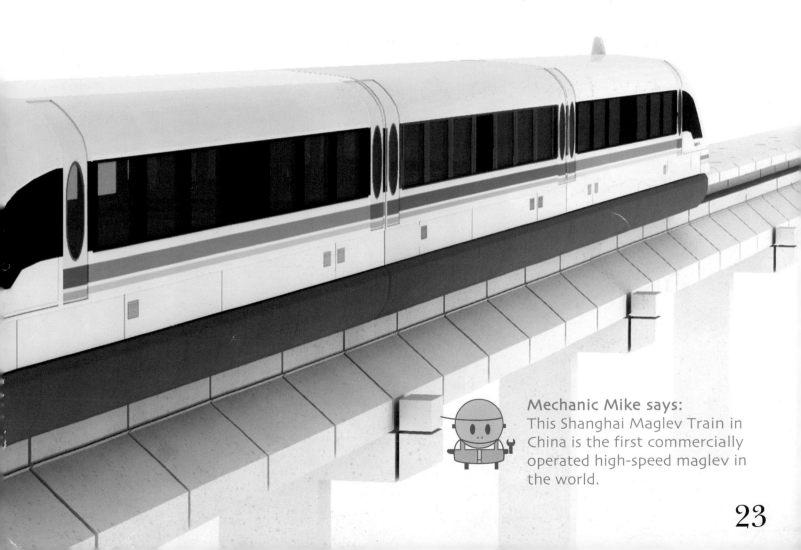

Mechanic Mike says:
This Shanghai Maglev Train in China is the first commercially operated high-speed maglev in the world.

Glossary

diesel
A fuel like gasoline used in diesel engines. Diesel engines can be very powerful.

electromagnet
A magnet produced using electricity.

elevated
Higher than the surrounding area.

locomotive
The railway vehicle that pulls a train.

rapid transit system
A rail passenger transport system in an urban area.

urban
A built-up area such as a city or town.

Index